Exploring Science

The Solar System

Exploring Science

The Solar System

Bradford Burnham

Thomson Learning
New York

A FRIEDMAN GROUP BOOK

First published in the
United States in 1995 by
Thomson Learning
New York, NY

Library of Congress Cataloging-in-Publication Data
  Burnham, Bradford, date
     The solar system and beyond / Bradford Burnham.
        p. cm. — (Exploring science)
     Includes bibliographical references and index.
     ISBN 1-56847-271-4
     1. Astronomy—Juvenile literature. 2. Astronomy—
  Experiments—Juvenile literature. [1. Astronomy. 2. Astronomy—
  Experiments. 3. Experiments.] I. Title. II. Series: Exploring
  science (New York, N.Y.)
  QB46.B94   1995
  520—dc20
                                            94-44416
                                               CIP
                                                AC

EXPLORING SCIENCE: THE SOLAR SYSTEM
was prepared and produced by
Michael Friedman Publishing Group, Inc.
15 West 26th Street
New York, New York 10010

Editor: Benjamin Boyington
Art Director/Designer: Jeff Batzli
Layout: Jonathan Gaines
Photography Director: Christopher Bain
Photography Editors: Christopher Bain,
Susan Mettler, and Wendy Missan
Illustrations: Brian Sullivan

Front Cover Illustration: George Gilliland
Back Cover Photographs courtesy NASA

Color separations by Benday Scancolour Co. Ltd.
Printed in China.

Dedication
To my father, for his fascination with life's mysteries

Acknowledgments
The author would like to thank many people
for their various contributions to this book:
Thomson Learning and the staff at the Michael Friedman
Publishing Group, especially Kelly Matthews, Ben
Boyington, and Jeff Batzli; the illustrators whose talent
gave dazzle to this book; Amy Gallagher and Brian
Sullivan, for their knowledge and support;
and finally, Lisa Sita, Karen Lund, Edward Dee, Ken Howell,
Amy Van Allen, and all my friends whose help and support
were as necessary to the completion of this book
as were pen and paper.

TABLE OF CONTENTS

INTRODUCTION

MYSTERIES IN THE SKY

ALTHOUGH WE KNOW A GREAT DEAL ABOUT THE PINPRICKS OF LIGHT IN OUR NIGHT SKY, THERE IS STILL A LOT OF MYSTERY SURROUNDING THESE FARAWAY OBJECTS.

Why Do Stars Twinkle?

Stars twinkle because of air. When their light travels through Earth's atmosphere, it passes through patches of hot and cold air that change its path just a little bit. This slight change causes the light to wobble, making it seem that the star is twinkling.

Our sky is filled with wonders. The Sun shines down on us during the day, and the Moon and stars sparkle at night. These objects and the others that inhabit outer space are called **celestial bodies**. Through the ages, people have looked up into the sky and wondered about these shining objects. Thousands of years ago, people did not have telescopes or other special instruments that would enable them to see faraway objects, so they could only create theories and discuss those celestial bodies that they could see with the naked eye. Because these ancient stargazers did not understand what they saw, they invented numerous myths and legends to explain what happened in the sky. Many civilizations believed that the celestial bodies were gods. To the early Egyptians, the Sun was the god Ra, who would sail across the sky each day in a giant boat.

PEOPLE HAVE STUDIED AND WOR-
SHIPED THE STARS AND OTHER
CELESTIAL BODIES FOR THOUSANDS
OF YEARS. THE ANCIENT EGYPTIANS
ARE WELL KNOWN FOR THEIR STAR-
GAZING. BELOW: AN EGYPTIAN
ASTRONOMER VIEWS THE NIGHT
SKY. RIGHT: THE FALCON-HEADED
SUN GOD RA WITH HIS SACRED
SYMBOL, THE SOLAR DISK.

The Legendary Milky Way

All the stars that we see with the naked eye are part of the Milky Way galaxy. Many of these stars form a dim streak across the sky. This band of stars is the heart of our galaxy, the Milky Way. There have been many myths and legends about the Milky Way. The Inuits, native people of the Arctic, believe that these stars are the snowshoe tracks of their legendary Raven. Native Americans living on the plains of the American Midwest believe that the Milky Way is a cloud of dust kicked up by a buffalo and a wildcat as they race across the sky.

Moving Stars

Although the stars seem to move, it is actually the Earth that moves. The Earth spins like a top, or rotates, making one full rotation every twenty-four hours. For about half those hours we are facing away from the Sun and are able to see the stars. To record the rotation of the Earth, take a picture of the stars. Have an adult help you with this activity. You will need warm clothes, a watch, low-speed film, a tripod or other method of keeping a camera still for a long period of time, and a camera with a shutter that can be kept open for minutes at a time (a fully automatic camera will not be appropriate for this activity).

1. On a clear, moonless night, go to an area where there are few lights (it would be even better if there were *no* lights in the area). Set up the tripod, set the focus on long range—the ∞ symbol (infinity)—and point the camera at the stars. If you have a cable shutter release for the camera, it will help to prevent jiggles.

2. Take many pictures; set the camera for different exposures and point it in different directions. Try taking photographs with the shutter kept open for varying lengths of time: a few seconds, about a minute, several minutes, an hour, many hours. The longer you leave the shutter open, the more star movement will be visible when you develop your pictures.

IN THIS PHOTOGRAPH, THE NORTH STAR (TOP OF PICTURE, NEAR TREETOP) SEEMS NOT TO HAVE MOVED EVEN THOUGH THE SHUTTER WAS LEFT OPEN FOR MANY HOURS. BECAUSE OF THIS STAR'S POSITION ABOVE THE NORTH POLE (WHICH IS EARTH'S AXIS OF RO-TATION), THE NORTH STAR MAKES A VERY SMALL CIRCLE THAT IS HARD TO DETECT.

ANCIENT PEOPLES AROUND THE WORLD BUILT SOME STRANGE AND BEAUTI- FUL STRUCTURES THAT WE BELIEVE WERE USED TO STUDY OR SHOW RESPECT FOR THE STARS. BELOW: STONEHENGE IN ENGLAND. BOTTOM: THE TEMPLE OF KUKULKAN, A MAYA PYRAMID IN SOUTHEASTERN MEXICO.

observe the movements of the Sun, the Moon, and the stars. The same is believed of the pyramids built by the Maya civilization of Mexico and Central America. The Mayas, whose society was at its peak from A.D. 300 to 800, were renowned for their observations of the heavens, which they used as the basis for a highly accurate calendar.

Thousands of years ago, the Babylonians created a system of mathematics to study the movements of the stars and planets. Their math is similar to modern-day algebra, and many of its features are still used today. The Babylonians developed the 360-degree circle, the sixty-minute hour, and the sixty-second minute.

According to these ancient civilizations' mythologies, the Sun, the Moon, and the stars were divine beings who were able to control the lives of humans and all the other creatures on Earth (not to mention weather, earthquakes, volcanic eruptions, and other natural phenomena). Because of this belief, the activities of these "gods" were studied very closely.

Scientists believe that Stonehenge, a monument in England that was built about 3,000 years ago, was designed as a sort of observatory—it is thought that Stonehenge's stone slabs were placed in a pattern that would allow people to

A Trillion Points of Light

Astronomers believe that there are about 100 billion galaxies in the universe. Since just one galaxy may have millions of stars, there may be close to 200 billion billion stars in the universe!

ASTRONOMY

The study of celestial bodies and the space they inhabit, known as the **universe**, is called **astronomy**. Scientists who study the universe to help us understand it better are called **astronomers**.

Astronomy was first organized as a science by the ancient Greeks, who used observations made by the Babylonians as well as observations of their own to develop theories about how Earth and its surrounding celestial bodies were

structured and how they work. While astronomers today can observe objects all over the universe, the original astronomers could see only the Moon, the Sun, and five nearby planets.

Pythagoras, a Greek mathematician and astronomer who lived in the sixth century B.C., was one of the first thinkers to put forth the theory that the Earth was round. While studying the movement of

THE LARGE TELESCOPES IN OBSERVATORIES, SUCH AS THE LICK OBSERVATORY ON MT. HAMILTON IN CALIFORNIA (ABOVE), ALLOW SCIENTISTS AND AMATEUR ASTRONOMERS THE OPPORTUNITY TO STUDY DIM AND DISTANT CELESTIAL BODIES.

the Moon, he had noticed that the shadow that the Earth occasionally left on the Moon was curved. This led him to believe that the Earth was a sphere. Unfortunately, this theory did not become widely accepted until the fifteenth or sixteenth century.

The belief that the Earth was flat was not the only misconception that was widely accepted as truth for hundreds of years. Until the 1500s, it was commonly believed that the Earth was the center of the universe (this is called the **geocentric** theory). Some time between 1520 and 1540, the Polish priest **Nicolaus Copernicus** put forth the daring theory that the planets revolved around the Sun, not around the Earth (this is called the **heliocentric theory**). Copernicus based this theory on his discovery that the movements of the planets fit better into a model that had the Sun as its center than one that was centered around the Earth. It was very difficult for people to believe this theory because it made the Earth seem less important than the Sun, and human pride made it hard to accept that the planet they lived on was not the center of the universe. This is only one of several important contributions Copernicus made to the science of astronomy.

THROUGHOUT HISTORY, MANY BRILLIANT THINKERS, SUCH AS THE SIXTH-CENTURY B.C. MATHEMATICIAN PYTHAGORAS (LEFT) AND THE SIXTEENTH-CENTURY PRIEST COPERNICUS (ABOVE), HAVE WORKED OUT VERY DIFFICULT AND TIME-CONSUMING CALCULATIONS TO FIND EVIDENCE FOR THEIR THEORIES ABOUT OUR SOLAR SYSTEM.

Sky Detective Journal

If you are truly serious about your star-gazing, you may want to create a journal in which you can record all the fun and fascinating things that you see during your nights of astronomical investigation. Over a month, a season, or a year, there are many things to learn about. By keeping a journal you will have a record of all that you saw, and if you have questions about what you observed you can take your journal with you when you go to ask a parent, teacher, or local astronomy expert about some of the things you saw.

1. Make the journal with the help of an adult. You will need some 8½-by-11-inch (21.5-by-27.9-centimeter) blank (or lined) white paper (enough for at least a month's worth of notes and drawings), one piece of construction paper (the color is up to you), yarn, crayons, and a hole punch.

2. Stack all your white paper, then fold the stack in half; fold the construction paper over this stack to make the cover. To bind the white paper and the construction paper together, punch two holes near the fold, string the yarn through the two holes, and tie the ends together. To complete your Sky Detective Journal, write your name and draw a picture on the cover.

On clear nights, go to a field or a large backyard away from town lights and observe the celestial bodies. Be sure an adult goes along. In addition to your journal, you may want to bring a friend, a flashlight (cover the top with a piece of red cellophane so that your night vision is not ruined by the white light), lawn chairs, blankets, hot chocolate, binoculars (or a telescope, if you have one), and a star-finder guidebook. Record all the interesting things that you see: shooting stars, satellites, planets, constellations, the Moon as it goes through its different phases, the Milky Way. You should write down any questions you have as they occur to you. You may even want to draw the various things that you see in the night sky, so if you go to an expert to ask questions you can show him or her what you're asking about. You can share your findings with your family, your friends, and even the members of your local astronomy club.

Thinkers such as Pytha-goras and Copernicus are just two of the many people who are famous for their studies of the sky. There are many more people from the past and the present who have also contributed to our knowledge of the universe. Astronomy is an ever-changing science—we are constantly making new discoveries and deepening our understanding of the heavens.

Night Light

When you go out at night to look at the stars, put a piece of red cellophane over the top of your flashlight. This way, your night vision will not be affected, but you will be able to see the ground and the area around you so you won't trip or run into anything. Because your eyes adjust to the amount of light around you, a flash-light shining a bright white light would change your vision from night to day, and you would not be able to see the faint stars until the white light was off and your eyes had adjusted to the darkness.

THE CONSTELLATIONS

There are many constella-tions in our night sky. For most people, a constellation is a group of stars that forms a star picture, such as Orion the Hunter or Ursa Major (which means "Great Bear" in Latin). For astron-omers, a constellation is also the area of the sky that contains the star pic-ture as well as the sur-rounding stars. There are a total of eighty-eight constellations (that is, areas of the sky), each of which

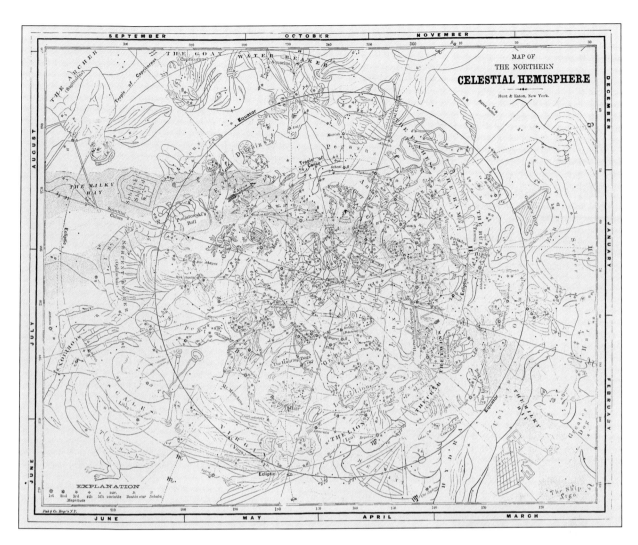

contains a specific star picture. These star pictures represent gods, heroes, animals, and tools that were significant to the ancient peoples who first observed them, and each has its own fascinating story or myth. Some examples of interesting star pictures include Andromeda (the Princess), Sagitta (the Arrow), and Telescopium (the Telescope).

One of the most easily seen images in our night sky, the Big Dipper, is not itself a constellation, but is part of the constellation Ursa Major. In one Native American myth the Big Dipper represents a bear that is being chased by three hunters. The hunter closest to the bear is carrying a bow and arrow; the second hunter is carrying a cooking pot; and the third hunter is collecting and carrying firewood. The hunters chase the bear through the sky all spring and summer until they are able to kill it in autumn. The bear's blood spills out from the heavens and stains the leaves of the

AN 1880S MAP OF THE CONSTELLATIONS OF THE NORTHERN HEMISPHERE. FOR MANY CONSTELLATIONS, THE STARS MAKE UP ONLY A PART OF THE STAR PICTURE— YOU HAVE TO USE YOUR IMAGINATION TO FILL IN THE REST. BECAUSE OF THIS, THEY CAN BE DIFFICULT TO IDENTIFY WITHOUT A GOOD FIELD GUIDE.

DURING ANY GIVEN NIGHT, WE ARE ABLE TO SEE ONLY A FEW OF THE MANY CONSTELLATIONS. WE SEE DIFFERENT CONSTELLATIONS DEPENDING ON THE SEASON AND OUR LOCATION ON EARTH. AT RIGHT ARE FOUR VIEWS OF THE NIGHT SKY. RIGHT, TOP: NORTHERN HEMISPHERE, SUMMER. RIGHT, BOTTOM: NORTHERN HEMISPHERE, WINTER. FAR RIGHT, TOP: SOUTHERN HEMISPHERE, SUMMER. FAR RIGHT, BOTTOM: SOUTHERN HEMISPHERE, WINTER.

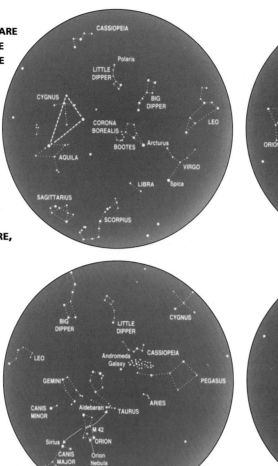

The North Star

The Little Dipper, a smaller version of the Big Dipper, is also a well-known star picture. The North Star is a semi-bright star at the end of the Little Dipper's handle. This star is named Polaris because it is found almost directly above the Earth's North Pole. Because of its location, Polaris seems to stay still in the sky as the Earth spins beneath it. All the other stars, though, seem to move across the sky during the night. Before compasses were invented, sailors and other explorers used the North Star to determine which direction was north. Of course, if the night was cloudy, they were out of luck.

trees red. The bear's skeleton can be seen in the winter sky. In the spring, the bear comes back to life and the chase begins anew.

Another well-known star picture is Orion the Hunter. Orion, which is visible in the Northern Hemisphere from November through March, has more bright stars than any other constellation. According to Greek mythology, Orion was a great hunter who was killed by the goddess Artemis. She loved him, but was tricked into killing him by her brother, the Sun god Apollo, who

was upset with Artemis for spending too much time on Earth with the mortal Orion. Apollo challenged his sister to an archery contest and pointed to a faraway target. Although Artemis could barely see the target, she knew that she could easily hit it. After firing her first arrow, she went to the target to see how true her aim had been, only to discover that she had killed her friend! Since she could not bring Orion back to life, she made his memory live forever by placing him in the skies.

Constellation Cup

With the help of an adult, create a constellation that you can show to other people. You will need a clean tin can with its top and bottom removed, black construction paper, scissors, tape, and a pin or sewing needle.

1. Cover the inside and outside of the can with black construction paper. Beware of sharp edges. Do not cover the openings.

2. Trace around the end of the can to make a circle on another piece of black construction paper, then draw a constellation inside the circle. Decide where the stars of the constellation will be and mark the locations with small dots.

3. Ask an adult to help you use the pin or needle to punch small holes through the paper where you have placed your stars. Cut out the circle of black construction paper and tape it to one end of the can.

4. Point the covered end of the can toward a light source and look into the open end. You should be able to see your constellation. If the constellation is not clear, try making the holes a little bigger. When you are satisfied with your constellation, show it to your friends and family.

5. To make your constellation even more interesting, try making up a legend about it. Tell this legend to your family and friends as they look into the can.

Sharing the Experience

There are many amateur astronomers throughout the world. Check your phone book to see if there is an astronomy club near you where you can share your enthusiasm about the sky with other people. The wonders that you will discover by stargazing and sharing your discoveries with others could entertain and amaze you for the rest of your life.

A PLANETARIUM IS A GREAT PLACE TO LEARN ABOUT THE STARS, THE CONSTELLATIONS, AND THE CHANGES THAT TAKE PLACE IN OUR SKY THROUGHOUT THE YEAR.

CHAPTER ONE

BIRTH OF A SOLAR SYSTEM

AN ARTIST'S CONCEPTION OF THE SOLAR SYSTEM'S FIRST FOUR PLANETS, A COMET, AND THEIR ORBITS AROUND THE SUN.

The planet Earth is one of many planets and moons that make up our solar system. A solar system is what astronomers call a group of planets and other objects that travel around a star. These objects are held in **orbit** (the path taken by one celestial body as it travels around another) by force of **gravity**.

The star that is the center of our solar system is called the Sun, and Earth is only one member of its "family" of orbiting objects. In our Sun's family there are nine planets, at least sixty-one moons, and many pieces of rock and ice. Is our solar system one of a kind? No one knows for sure. Astronomers are still seeking the answer to this question, and one day they may discover that our solar system is not unique and that many of the stars we can see from Earth also have families of orbiting objects.

Heavy Stuff

Have you ever wondered why we stay on Earth instead of floating into space? We are held to the surface of Earth by gravity, a force of attraction that pulls us toward Earth's center. Humans also have gravity; in fact, all objects have gravity. The strength of an object's gravity is based on its mass. Because Earth's force of gravity is a lot stronger than that of a human, it is nearly impossible for us to feel our own forces of gravity.

THE BEGINNING

Astronomers who study the origin of the universe are called **cosmologists**. These scientists have been studying the stars and planets for centuries, hoping to learn how our solar system (and the universe) was born and how it became what it is today. One of the most widely accepted explanations is the **big bang theory**.

According to the big bang theory, the universe began as a ball of material called the **primeval atom**. Everything in the universe today (the stars, the planets, and even people) is made of material that was once inside this large ball. Cosmologists believe that about fifteen billion years ago this large ball exploded, sending matter and energy flying in all directions. Slowly, over millions of years, the material from the big bang started to gather together into large clouds. These large clouds eventually developed into what we know as **galaxies**. Inside these developing galaxies were the building materials for all the stars and planets that exist today.

AN ARTIST'S CONCEPTION OF THE BIG BANG, WHICH IS BELIEVED TO HAVE TAKEN PLACE ABOUT FIFTEEN BILLION YEARS AGO.

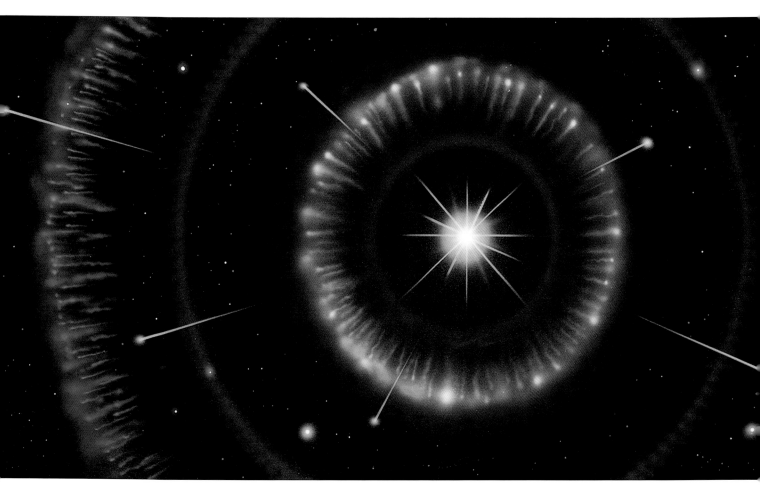

Naming the Galaxies

Most of the time, galaxies are not named. Astronomers usually give them numbers. A few galaxies, though, are named for what they look like—the Black Eye, the Whirlpool, the Sombrero, and the Milky Way.

ABOVE: ASTRONOMERS HAVE DISCOVERED MANY GALAXIES BESIDES OUR OWN. THE MILLIONS OF STARS THAT MAKE UP THESE GALAXIES SOMETIMES FORM RECOGNIZABLE SHAPES. SOME GALAXIES, LIKE OUR OWN MILKY WAY, SEEM TO BE SPIRAL IN SHAPE (LEFT); OTHERS ARE ELLIPTICAL, OR OVAL (MIDDLE); AND STILL OTHERS HAVE NO RECOGNIZABLE PATTERN AT ALL AND ARE CALLED IRREGULAR (RIGHT).

GALAXIES

Galaxies come in many different shapes and sizes. Their different shapes are the result of the movements of the clouds of gases and cosmic dust (tiny particles, usually made of carbon, that measure $^{25}/_{1000}$ inch [0.6 millimeters] or less) inside them. These movements are caused by the gravitational forces within each galaxy. Astronomers believe that the center of each galaxy has very strong gravity—so strong, in fact, that everything within the galaxy is constantly being pulled toward its center. A pattern of movement is sometimes created as every-

thing moves around and toward the galaxy's center. Astronomers have found three kinds of patterns: **spiral**, **elliptical**, and **irregular**. Spiral galaxies are shaped like the spirals that form as water goes down a drain. Elliptical galaxies are shaped like a large flattened oval disk. And irregular galaxies come in many shapes—there is no regular pattern to their internal movements. Our solar system is part of a galaxy called the Milky Way, a spiral galaxy, which, like other spiral galaxies, has many long arms that reach out into space. Our Sun is located in one of the Milky Way's arms, along with thousands of other stars.

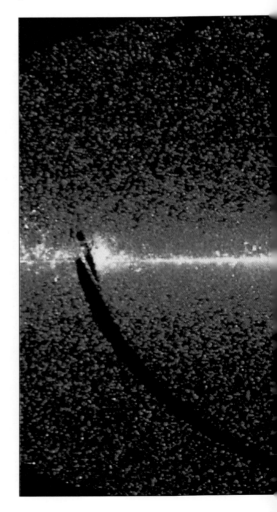

Growing Universe

In 1912 American astronomers discovered that other galaxies in the universe were moving away from our galaxy very quickly. At that time no one knew what this meant, but today we know it means the universe is growing in size. Will it ever stop expanding? Astronomers have not yet found the answer, but they are still investigating.

WITH THIS COMPOSITE PHOTOGRAPH (A SPECIAL PICTURE CREATED BY PUTTING TOGETHER SEVERAL PHOTOGRAPHIC IMAGES) OF THE MILKY WAY GALAXY, WE ARE ABLE TO SEE ALL THE STARS WE WOULD NORMALLY SEE OVER THE COURSE OF MANY NIGHTS COLLECTED IN ONE IMAGE. THE BRIGHT BAND THAT STRETCHES ACROSS THE CENTER OF THE PICTURE CONTAINS THE STARS THAT MAKE UP THE CENTER AND ARMS OF THE MILKY WAY.

STAR NURSERIES

Within galaxies there are clouds of gases and dust called nebulae (the plural form of the word **nebula**, which in Latin means "mist" or "cloud"). Astronomers believe that stars are made of the material inside these clouds; because of this, nebulae have been nicknamed "star nurseries." It is believed that one nebula can give rise to thousands of stars over a long period of time. Stars are created as gases and dust, attracted by gravity, come together within the nebula and form large spinning balls. As a star forms, however, not all of the gases and dust are pulled into the developing star; sometimes they form into a donut-shaped ring of debris circling the new star.

ASTRONOMERS BELIEVE THAT THE CLOUDS OF GASES AND DUST INSIDE NEBULAE (ABOVE AND BELOW) ABSORB AND REFLECT THE LIGHT FROM SURROUNDING STARS, RESULTING IN BEAUTIFULLY COLORED "STAR NURSERIES" LIKE THESE.

History in the Sky

Some stars are so far away from Earth that it takes thousands or even millions of years for their light to reach us. For example, the Crab Nebula in the constellation Taurus is 6,000 light-years away (a **light-year** is the distance light travels in one year: about 6 trillion miles [9.6 trillion kilometers]); therefore, the light we see that comes from the Crab Nebula is about 6,000 years old. Some stars are even farther away; astronomers have discovered a few that may be as much as 15 billion light-years away!

AN ARTIST'S CONCEPTION OF A STAR AND THE DUST, GASES, AND PLANETS THAT MIGHT SURROUND IT.

SOLAR SYSTEMS

Astronomers believe that planets and moons are formed from the leftover material surrounding a new star. Hydrogen and nitrogen gases and small pieces of rock, ice, and dust travel around the new star in many different paths and at many different speeds. As these objects move around in this cloud of material, there are many collisions. Some objects are knocked out of the solar system, while others crash into each other and combine to form larger objects. After many collisions, these combinations of rock, ice, and dust may become large enough to be considered planets. Astronomers believe that this is how Earth and the other planets formed.

How Old Is the Solar System?

Astronomers believe that our Sun and the planets that surround it are about five billion years old. While this seems quite old, our Sun is actually rather young compared to other stars in the universe. Many stars are billions of years older than the Sun, and some of these are now dead or dying. Our Sun, however, will continue to shine for at least another five billion years.

AN ILLUSTRATION OF HOW THE INNER PLANETS MAY HAVE LOOKED BILLIONS OF YEARS AGO, DURING THE EARLY STAGES OF OUR SOLAR SYSTEM'S DEVELOPMENT.

While astronomers have learned a great deal about the origins of the solar system and the universe over the centuries, there is still much to learn. Research intended to help us better understand the processes involved in the formation and continual change of celestial bodies is ongoing, and scientists frequently discover new events, or **phenomena,** in the universe. Recently, evidence pointing to the existence of another solar system in space was discovered. Although astronomers are not yet certain that this other solar system exists, the mere possibility of its existence is very exciting. One day it may be discovered that many of the stars we can see in our night sky are orbited by families of planets and moons, just as our star— the Sun—is orbited by the planets and moons in our solar system.

Searching for Solar Systems

Astronomers have recently discovered that a certain faraway star seems to be orbited by two planet-size objects. This exciting news lends support to the theory that our Sun is not unique and that many stars in the universe have planets.

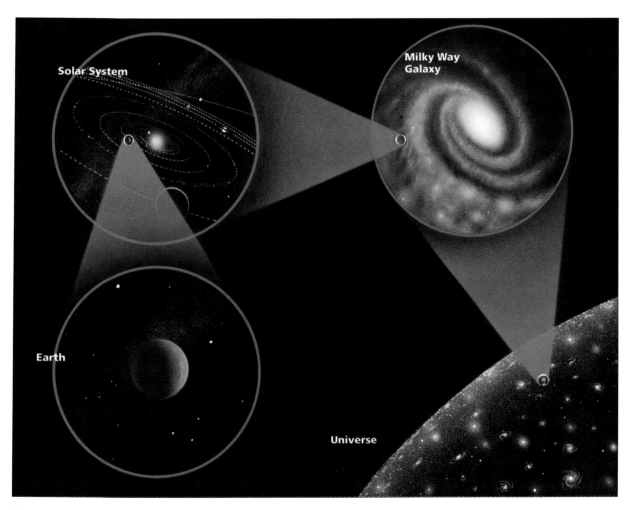

AN ILLUSTRATION OF OUR PLACE IN THE UNIVERSE, BASED ON WHAT ASTRONOMERS THROUGHOUT HISTORY HAVE LEARNED ABOUT THE VASTNESS WE CALL SPACE.

CHAPTER TWO

THE SUN

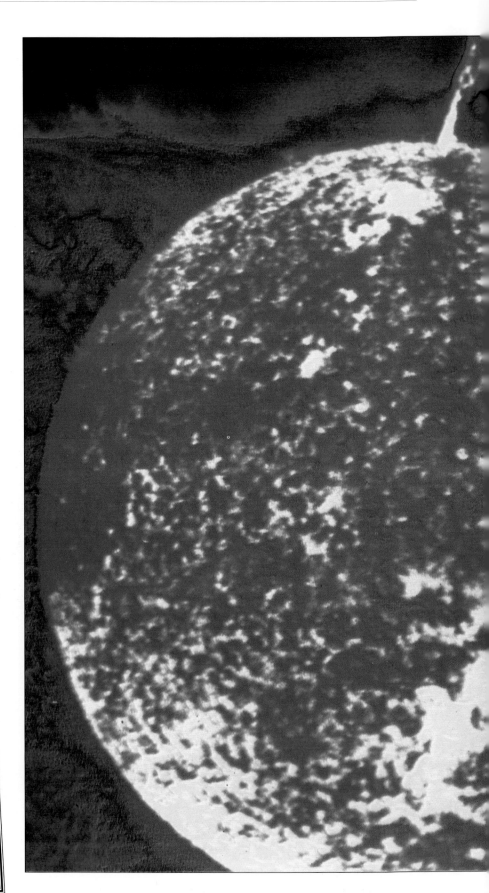

At the center of our solar system is a star that we know as the Sun. This star provides the warmth and light that plants and animals need to survive. Without the heat and light of the Sun, life on Earth would probably never have developed. But what exactly is the Sun? How does it work? And how long will it shine? For thousands of years astronomers have been trying to answer these questions, and they have developed numerous theories about the Sun and about stars in general.

The Mass of It All

The Sun contains more than 99 percent of the mass of our entire solar system. In fact, the Sun is so large that a million Earths could fit inside it.

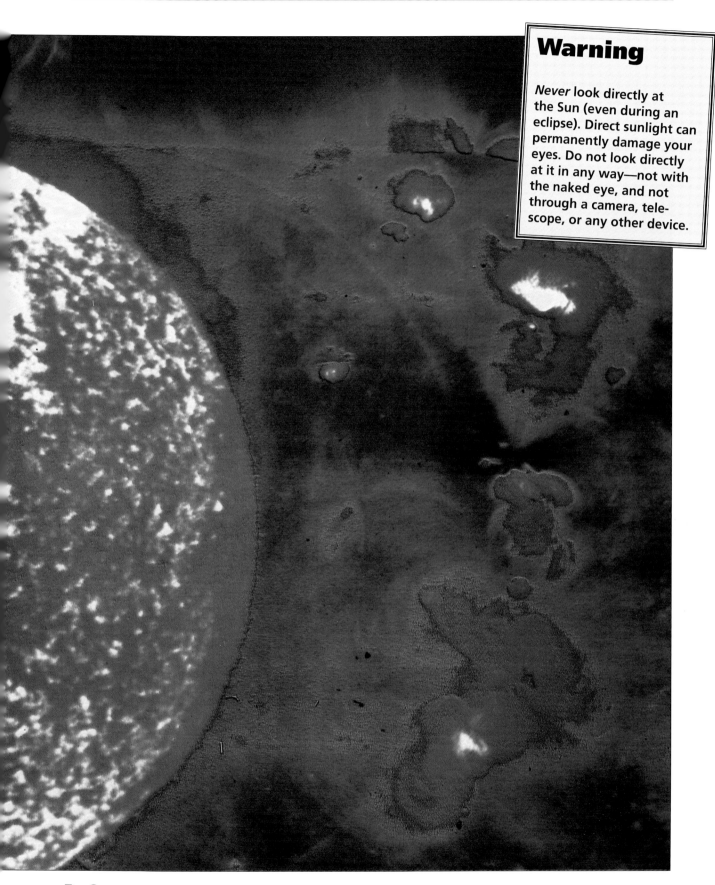

THE SUN **EMITS**, OR RELEASES, ENERGY IN MANY SPECTACULAR WAYS; **SOLAR FLARES**, LIKE THE ONE VISIBLE AT THE TOP OF THIS PHOTOGRAPH, ERUPT FROM THE SUN'S SURFACE AND REACH THOUSANDS OF MILES INTO SPACE.

Binary Stars

A **binary star**, or **binary system**, is a system of two stars, held together by gravity, that revolve around each other. Astronomers have two theories about how binary stars are formed. According to the first, one star gets too close to another and their gravities trap them in orbit around each other. In the second theory, the donut-shaped cloud of material surrounding a new star (the material left over from when the star was originally formed) forms a second star. If the new star is large enough, the two will fall into orbit around each other.

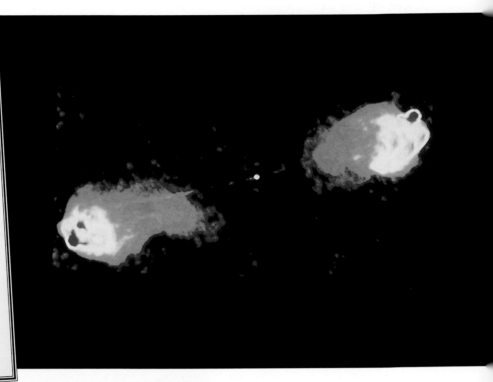

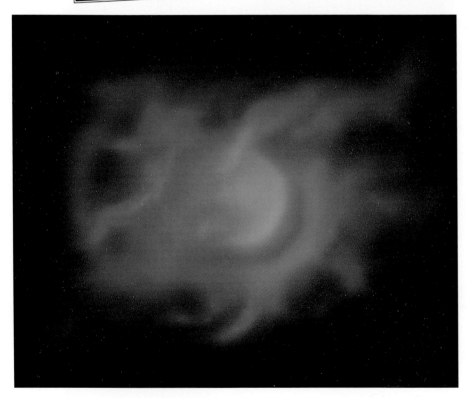

AN ARTIST'S CONCEPTION OF A PROTOSTAR.

BIRTH OF A STAR

Stars form as the gases and dust that make up nebulae slowly come together to make a tight, spinning ball of energy called a **protostar**. As the molecules of gas and dust within the protostar bump into each other, the developing star begins to generate heat. If enough heat is generated to produce **nuclear fusion reactions**, the protostar becomes a star.

Nuclear fusion reactions occur in the center of a star, called the **core**, where temperatures can reach

From the Inside Out

Before the energy that is generated in a star's core reaches the surface, it makes a long journey through the many layers of the star. The first layer from the core is called the **radiation zone**; it is so thick that it may take millions of years for the core's energy to pass through it. The second layer is called the **convection zone**. This layer is in constant motion as energy travels through it, creating large bubbles of gases. The third layer is called the **photosphere**. This is actually the lower layer of the sun's atmosphere; it is the layer we see. It is from this layer that energy is released into space. Sometimes the energy bursts out of the photosphere and creates large eruptions (depending on the shape they take and how long they last, these eruptions are called **spicules, flares,** or **prominences**). These eruptions occur in or near the outermost layer of a star, called the **chromosphere.**

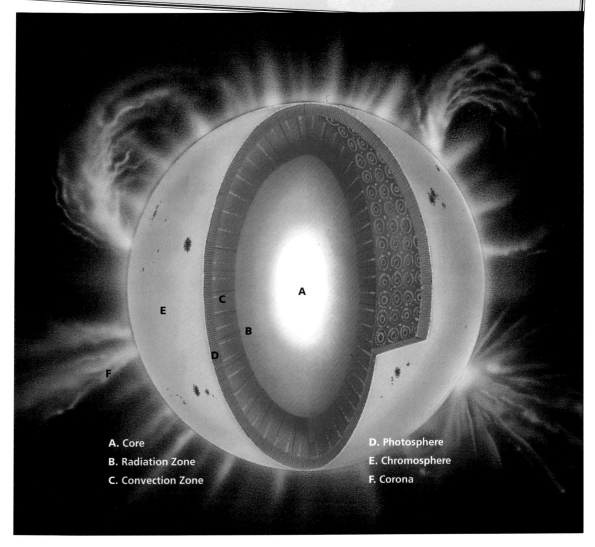

A. Core
B. Radiation Zone
C. Convection Zone
D. Photosphere
E. Chromosphere
F. Corona

more than 27,000,000°F (15,000,000°C), which is about equal to the heat generated by 100 million hydrogen bombs being set off at once. These reactions occur as four hydrogen atoms combine to form one helium atom. This fusion produces a lot of energy, and it is this energy that gives a star its glow.

DEATH OF A STAR

Eventually, after millions of years, stars run out of fuel. The Sun has been burning for about five billion years, and it will continue to burn for about another five billion years. Someday, though, the hydrogen fuel inside the Sun will run out.

As stars begin running out of fuel, they go through a series of changes in temperature and size. A star the size of the Sun will collapse in on itself when the fuel runs out. The pressure and heat that build up inside a star as it collapses cause a burst of nuclear fusion reactions. This burst expands the star so that it becomes many times its original size. As the star begins to cool, its color changes from yellow to red; at this stage, it is called a **red giant**. Eventually, red giants use up their remaining fuel and shrink until they are about the size of Earth. At this point, the star has so little energy that it gives off only a faint white light; the star is now called a **white dwarf**. When the white dwarf uses up the rest of its fuel, it stops shining altogether; in this final stage, the star is called a **black dwarf**.

AN ILLUSTRATION SHOWING THE RELATIVE SIZES OF KNOWN TYPES OF STARS. OUR SUN WILL REMAIN A YELLOW STAR FOR ABOUT ANOTHER FIVE BILLION YEARS.

THESE BEFORE-AND-AFTER PICTURES ILLUSTRATE THE DRAMATIC CHANGES THAT OCCUR WHEN A STAR GOES SUPERNOVA.

Some larger stars have a much more spectacular finish to their lives. **Blue giants** usually use up their hydrogen fuel more quickly than other kinds of stars. Their lifespans range from a few million to a few billion years, which is actually a very short period of time on the cosmic scale. As a blue giant "dies," it also expands, becoming a very large star called a **red supergiant**. The red super-

Supernova in the Sky

In the year 1054 a supernova was discovered in the constellation Taurus. It was very bright and could be seen with the naked eye even during the day. Over time the debris slowly lost its brightness and became a glowing cloud of gas and dust particles. This cloud of debris is known as the Crab Nebula, and with the help of a telescope it can still be seen today.

giant is not very stable, and it soon begins to contract, becoming smaller and smaller until the internal pressure builds up and

causes the star to explode. This stellar explosion, called a **supernova**, is very powerful and sends debris in all directions.

Neutron Stars

A neutron star is so dense that one teaspoon of its material weighs as much as one million tons (907,000 metric tons)! These stars cannot easily be seen, but they can be "heard." They emit radio waves that astronomers are able to pick up with their radio telescopes.

A small portion of this material, however, stays behind and becomes a very dense (meaning that it is very heavy for its size) spinning ball. This ball is called a **neutron star**, and its force of gravity is extremely strong.

Astronomers believe that some dying stars, instead of becoming neutron stars, turn into **black holes**, spinning balls that are even more dense than neutron stars and have forces of gravity so strong that not even light can escape their pull. Scientists have theorized that there are many black holes scattered across the universe, but the existence of these celestial phenomena is extremely hard to prove.

Evidence of Black Holes

The existence of black holes was originally predicted by the physicist Albert Einstein, who believed that there were a great many of them in the universe. Recent research has shown that there is a massive black hole in galaxy M87. Scientists discovered this by studying the gases spinning around the galaxy's center. According to data collected by instruments such as the **Hubble Space Telescope**, the mass of this black hole is equal to the mass of about two billion Suns.

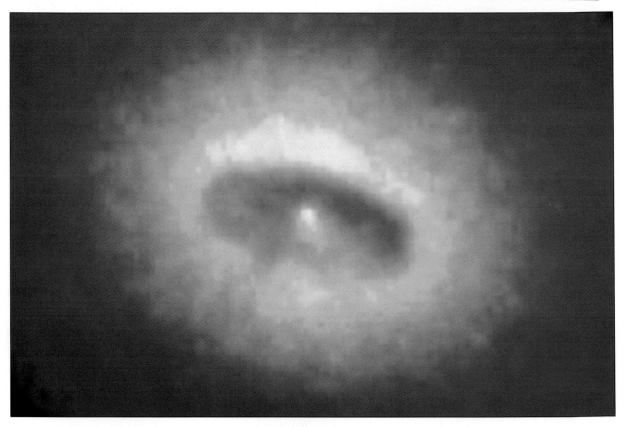

THE PATTERN OF STARS SURROUNDING A SUSPECTED BLACK HOLE (ABOVE) CAN SERVE AS EVIDENCE OF THE EXISTENCE OF THAT PHENOMENON. TO TRY TO PROVE THAT A PARTICULAR BLACK HOLE EXISTS, ASTRONOMERS OBSERVE THESE PATTERNS, APPLY VARIOUS MATHEMATIC PRINCIPLES, AND PERFORM NUMEROUS CALCULATIONS.

A Person-Year

The light that stars emit travels through space at about 186,000 miles (about 300,000 kilometers) per second. A light-year is the distance light travels in one year: about 6 trillion miles (about 9.6 trillion kilometers). For a fun math project, you might try figuring out how far you and your friends could walk in a year: a person-year.

You will need a watch with a second hand, a calculator, and a place where you can measure distance. A running track is an ideal place for this activity, but a football field or other place where you can measure walking distance will also do. If you are unable find a place for this activity, you can use a walking speed of 3 miles per hour (4.8 kilometers per hour) for the calculations.

Here are two ways to collect your data:

1. On a running track, record how many minutes it takes you to walk or run 1/8 mile. Round off the time to the nearest minute and multiply by 8. Now divide 60 (the number of minutes in an hour) by this new number. The result is your speed in miles per hour. (To figure your speed in kilometers per hour, walk the same distance—equal to 1/5 kilometer—then multiply by 5 the number of minutes it takes you and divide that number into 60.)

2. You might also calculate this number by walking or running the length of a football field. Record how many minutes it takes you to travel 100 yards (90 meters). Round off the time to the nearest minute, and since there are 1,760 yards in a mile, multiply your time by 17.6 to find out your speed in minutes per mile. Now divide 60 (the number of minutes in an hour) by this new number. The result is your speed in miles per hour. (To figure your speed in kilometers per hour, multiply by 1.61).

After you have figured out your speed in miles (or kilometers) per hour, it is time to calculate your person-year. Multiply your speed by 24 (the number of hours in a day), then multiply the new number by 365 (the number of days in a year). The result is your person-year.

SUNLIGHT

The Sun emits many different kinds of energy—X rays, microwaves, radio waves, and visible light. Astronomers study these energies, called the **electromagnetic spectrum**, to learn about the Sun and other stars. Studying these waves of energy reveals information about the sizes, ages, and interiors of stars.

Sunscreen

Some of the energies emitted by the sun, such as ultraviolet (UV) light, are harmful. While the Earth's atmosphere acts as a natural sunscreen, preventing some of these energies from reaching us, even on cloudy days some UV light gets through. UV light damages our skin cells, and when the cells are damaged we get sunburns. Our bodies produce a natural sunscreen, called **melanin,** that helps to prevent damage to our cells, but it is not always 100 percent effective. You can, however, buy commercial sunscreen in your local drugstore. Sunscreen was created to block as much UV light as possible from reaching our skin; the higher the number on the sunscreen, the more UV light it blocks.

WHITE LIGHT IS ACTUALLY A COMBINATION OF ALL THE COLORS SHOWN BY THIS PRISM. THE FULL SPECTRUM OF LIGHT INCLUDES THESE COLORS AND OTHER WAVELENGTHS OF ENERGY THAT OUR EYES CANNOT SEE.

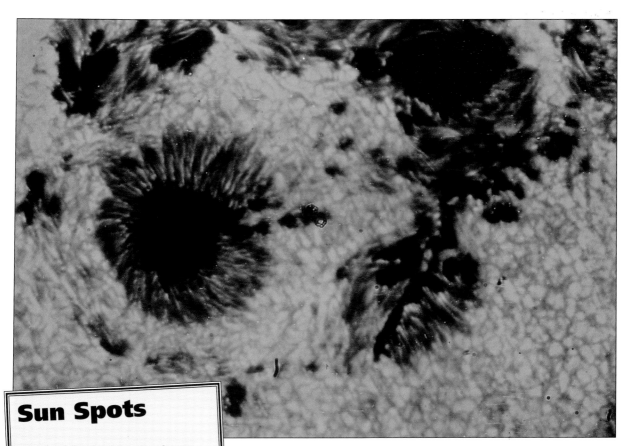

Sun Spots

Not all parts of the Sun's surface shine brightly. There are small dark areas that do not seem to be as hot as the rest of the Sun. These are called **sun spots**, and astronomers believe that they are cooler because they are areas of intense magnetic activity. Every eleven years, the Sun goes through a cycle of intense activity, and many sun spots are created. During these periods of heightened activity, the Sun emits more intense energy, and this energy disturbs communications, disorients birds, and may even change world weather conditions.

Although the Sun shines with a yellow light, not all stars in the universe are this color. The outer layer of a star is called the photosphere, and it is the temperature of this layer that determines the color of a star. Blue giants have very hot surfaces, about 55,000°F (31,000°C), and at these temperatures the light is blue. If, like the Sun, a star's surface has a temperature of about 14,500°F (about 8,000°C), then it shines with a yellow light. And if the surface is cooler, say about 5,500°F (about 3,000 °C), then the star shines with a red glow. The stars in our night sky are so far away, though, that for the most part we are unable to see their colors without a telescope or similar instrument.

It is important to remember that we are just beginning to understand the different kinds of energies that the Sun and stars emit and the reasons why they shine. Although we have learned a great deal over the years, there are still many questions to be answered.

Polar Lights

The northern lights (aurora borealis) and the southern lights (aurora australis) occur when charged particles from the Sun strike Earth's atmosphere. For the most part, Earth's magnetic field lets these particles enter the atmosphere only near the North and South poles, so it is only in the northernmost and southernmost areas of the world that they are visible. At night the polar skies can be filled with bands of waving blues, greens, oranges, and reds. According to one myth of the Naskapi Indians of Labrador, the northern lights are spirits dancing in the night sky.

Playing in a Rainbow

Astronomers use an instrument called a **spectroscope** to study the different types of energy found in sunlight. You can study some of these energies with a household item: a lawn sprinkler. As sunlight passes through water droplets, it is split into the different waves of energy that together make white light. We know these waves as the colors of the rainbow. The water droplets from the sprinkler and from passing sun showers break apart the white light to create a rainbow, which sometimes seems to stretch across the horizon.

CHAPTER THREE

THE SUN'S FAMILY

Earth is part of a family of celestial bodies that travel around the Sun. Other members of this family include Earth's moon, eight other planets and their moons, a number of comets, and many asteroids of varying size and shape. Each family member has its own unique characteristics and travels around the Sun in its own path, or orbit. Over the centuries, astronomers have made many interesting (and surprising) discoveries about the other members of the Sun's family, most of which are very different from Earth.

A COMPOSITE PHOTOGRAPH OF THE FIRST EIGHT OF THE NINE PLANETS IN OUR SOLAR SYSTEM, ALONG WITH THE EARTH'S MOON.

Imperfect Circles

An orbit is the path that an object takes as it travels around a star or other celestial body. In 1609 the German mathematician Johannes Kepler, shown above, published his discovery about the movements of the planets. After many experiments and calculations, he concluded that the planets traveled in elliptical orbits, not in circular orbits as was commonly believed. (An ellipse is a circle that bulges at both ends.) Some planets have orbits that are very nearly round, but none of them travel in a perfect circle.

THE INNER PLANETS

Many of the planets in our solar system can be seen in the night sky. These planets do not give off their own light—they reflect the light of the Sun. As they orbit the Sun, they move slowly among the stars and through the constellations. You cannot perceive their movement by looking at them, but if you check their location from night to night, you will see that they do indeed move. Ancient peoples did not know what these "traveling stars" were; the Greeks named them planets, which means "wanderers." Over the centuries, with the help of telescopes and other, more recently developed instruments, we have learned much more about them.

Most of the planets in our solar system are very different from Earth. Some of them have surfaces of rock, but these surfaces are jagged and dangerous. A few have atmospheres, though they are usually very thin and are made up of gases that are poisonous to human beings and other animals. The surface temperatures of the other planets also differ from that of Earth—they range from colder than the coldest freezer to much hotter than boiling water. The four planets closest to the Sun are called the **inner planets**.

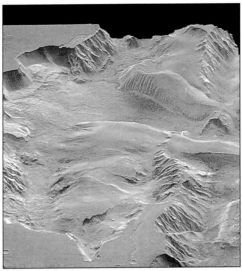

A COMPUTER-GENERATED IMAGE OF THE SURFACE OF **M**ARS, WHOSE GRAVITY IS EQUAL TO ABOUT FOUR-TENTHS THAT OF **E**ARTH.

Jumping Contest

The force of gravity on the other planets and their moons is not the same as that on Earth. Mercury's gravity, for instance, is less powerful than Earth's; on Mercury, you would weigh one-third of what you weigh on Earth and be able to jump about three times higher than you can here. On the Earth's moon, you would weigh one-sixth of your usual weight and be able to jump about six times as high as you can here. On Jupiter, however, you would weigh about twice as much as you normally do and be able to jump only about half as high, because its gravity is more than twice as strong as Earth's.

The planet closest to the Sun is called **Mercury**. This planet is very hard to see, but a skilled and patient sky-gazer can occasionally see it in the early morning or early evening. The planet was named after the Roman god Mercury, the swift messenger of the gods, because it travels across our sky faster than any other planet.

Because Mercury is so close to the Sun, its surface and thin atmosphere receive a great deal of heat, and the temperature can rise as high as 800°F (about 430°C). This heat, however, is quickly lost; at night, the temperature drops hundreds of degrees, to near –290°F (about –180°C).

MERCURY, THE CLOSEST PLANET TO THE SUN, IS LESS THAN HALF THE SIZE OF EARTH. WITH ALL ITS CRATERS, IT ALMOST LOOKS LIKE THE MOON.

IN OUR NIGHT SKY, VENUS IS THE BRIGHTEST OF THE PLANETS. ITS CLOUDS OF SULFURIC ACID REFLECT MUCH OF THE SUN'S LIGHT.

The second planet from the Sun is named **Venus**, after the Roman goddess of beauty. Venus is nicknamed the "Morning Star" or "Evening Star"—it can be seen most easily in the early morning and in the early evening.

Venus has a rocky surface and is about the same size as Earth, but it would be difficult to live there. The atmosphere is almost 95 percent carbon dioxide (Earth's atmosphere is less than 1 percent carbon dioxide). The carbon dioxide acts like a greenhouse, trapping the Sun's heat and raising the surface temperature to about 900°F (480°C), hot enough to melt lead. There is also a constant rain of sulfuric acid (a kind of acid that is highly corrosive, meaning it can make holes in wood, clothing, and you). This rain never reaches the ground, however, because it evaporates in the hot, dry atmosphere as it falls.

Earth, the third planet from the sun, has a very calm climate. We are familiar with Earth's climate, atmosphere, and surface, but until we compare them with those of the other planets we do not realize how unique they are. Earth's atmosphere traps enough of the Sun's heat to keep the surface temperature between −130°F (−90°C) and 136°F (58°C). These temperatures allow water to remain a liquid over much of the planet and life to flourish. As far as we know, there are no life-forms on any of the other planets.

Mars is the fourth planet from the Sun, and much like the Earth it has seasons. The temperature changes that occur during the Martian year cause the **polar ice caps**, which are made of water and carbon dioxide (dry ice), to shrink and expand much like the ice caps at Earth's North and South poles.

At one time it was believed that Mars had life. More than a hundred years ago, astronomers observed what looked like canals on its surface. At first, they believed that the canals were built by intelligent life to allow water to be transported from the polar ice caps to the rest of the planet. Years later, after further research and exploration via spacecraft that landed on the surface of Mars, astronomers concluded that the canals were not made by intelligent life-forms. They theorized that the canals may have been caused by the rushing

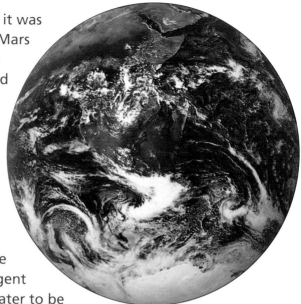

OUR MAJESTIC HOME: EARTH.

waters of streams and rivers that existed on the planet's surface long ago.

Mercury, Venus, Earth, and Mars are made mostly of metal and rock. These planets have cores of iron and other heavy elements that are surrounded by molten rock. The molten rock sometimes comes to the surface in the form of **lava**; when this lava reaches the surface it cools and becomes hard. The ground is a thin layer of cooled lava that floats on top of the molten rock underneath. Of the inner planets, only Earth has an abundance of water, which covers more than 70 percent of our planet's surface.

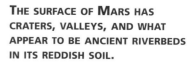

THE SURFACE OF MARS HAS CRATERS, VALLEYS, AND WHAT APPEAR TO BE ANCIENT RIVERBEDS IN ITS REDDISH SOIL.

Walk the Solar System

To understand the relative size of the solar system, try pacing out the relative distances between the planets with your family, friends, or classmates. You will need nine other people. (If possible, go to a football field, because it will help give a frame of reference; otherwise, use a large lawn or a long parking lot.) If you can't find anyone to join you and you decide to do this by yourself, you may want to make signs that you can place on the ground to represent the different planets.

To begin, ask someone to volunteer to be the Sun and have that person stand at one end of the field. Then ask each of the others to be a different planet, and have them stand at the specific distances listed below.

The distances between planets are as follows (scale: 1 foot [0.3 meters] = 12,000,000 miles [19,320,000 kilometers]):

Mercury	3 feet (0.9 meters) from the Sun
Venus	3 feet (0.9 meters) from Mercury
Earth	2 feet (0.6 meters) from Venus
Mars	4 feet (1.2 meters) from Earth
Jupiter	28 feet (8.4 meters) from Mars
Saturn	34 feet (10.2 meters) from Jupiter
Uranus	74 feet (22.2 meters) from Saturn
Neptune	84 feet (25.2 meters) from Uranus
Pluto	73 feet (21.9 meters) from Neptune

Remember that these numbers do not indicate each planet's distance from the Sun, but the planets' distances from each other.

Let everyone know that in this exercise they themselves are much larger in size than the planets they are representing. For example, at this scale the Sun is only 3/4 inch (1.9 centimeters) in diameter and Jupiter is less than 1/8 inch (0.3 centimeters) in diameter. Once everyone is in place, have each person, in turn, call out the name of the planet he or she is pretending to be.

THE OUTER PLANETS

Jupiter, **Saturn**, **Uranus**, **Neptune**, and **Pluto** are much farther away from the Sun and are separated from the inner planets by a wide strip of **asteroids**. These last five planets are called the **outer planets**.

Jupiter, Saturn, Uranus, and Neptune are made mostly of liquids and gases, instead of rock and metal. They do, however, have small rocky cores. These cores are surrounded by many layers of liquids and gases (hydrogen, helium, methane, and ammonia). The gases make colorful patterns as they are blown around the planets' atmospheres by violent storms. These large gaseous planets are surrounded by circles of debris that we call **rings**. These rings are made up of small particles of rock, ice, and dust that are held in orbit around the planets by gravity. Saturn has hundreds of rings, many of which can be seen with the help of a

METHANE IN ITS ATMOSPHERE GIVES URANUS A GREENISH COLOR.

telescope. Jupiter, Uranus, and Neptune, however, have fewer rings, and these rings are more difficult to see. Pluto has no rings.

Jupiter, the largest planet in our solar system, is the fifth from the Sun, after Mars. Jupiter was named after the Roman king of gods, because of its immense size. The diameter of Jupiter is more than ten times that of Earth, and scientists have calculated that more than one thousand Earths could fit inside this giant planet! Jupiter has many gaseous storms, which are caused by the planet's rapid rotation. These storms give Jupiter a very colorful and ever-shifting appearance. Jupiter's largest storm, the **Great Red Spot**, is the size of three Earths. This giant storm has been traveling through Jupiter's atmosphere for at least three hundred years.

Saturn, which is next after Jupiter, also has violent storms. These storms' winds can blow at speeds of up to 1,100 miles per hour (about 1,800 kilometers per hour). The most spectacular thing about Saturn, though, is its rings, which are made up of millions of pieces of dust and ice. The many rings surrounding Saturn are each only a mile (about 1.6 kilometers) or so thick,

but they reach more than 94,000 miles (about 151,000 kilometers) into space.

Uranus, the seventh planet from the sun, is unusual in that it lies on its side as it spins—its axis of rotation is at a 90° angle to its orbit. Astronomers believe that it rotates at this angle because many centuries ago a large object collided with the planet and pushed it onto its side. (Its rings also travel at a 90° angle to the orbit.) Because of the way Uranus spins, its days and nights are different at different times of the year. A day may last for eight hours during one part of the year and for many months at other parts of the year.

Neptune, the next planet after Uranus, is a cold and violent planet. Its atmosphere has a temperature of –261°F (about

TOP: JUPITER'S ATMOSPHERE IS MOSTLY HYDROGEN. THE MOST DISTINCT ELEMENT OF THIS PLANET'S ATMOSPHERE IS THE GREAT RED SPOT (WHICH YOU CAN SEE AT THE CENTER OF THE PLANET). ABOVE: SATURN'S WELL-KNOWN AND BEAUTIFUL RINGS ARE MADE UP OF DUST AND ICE THAT ORBIT THAT PLANET. THEIR COLOR IS ACTUALLY A REFLECTION OF THE SUN'S LIGHT.

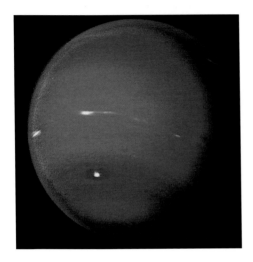

-163°C), and its winds blow at speeds of up to 1,500 miles per hour (about 2,400 kilometers per hour). Like Jupiter, Neptune has a large storm, called the **Great Dark Spot**, that is as large as the planet Earth.

The Farthest Planet

Pluto occasionally gives the title of farthest planet from the Sun to Neptune. Because of the odd shape of Pluto's orbit, this planet is sometimes quite far from the Sun and other times much closer. In 1979 Pluto's orbit brought it inside the orbit of Neptune. Neptune will keep the title of farthest planet until 1999, when Pluto's orbit will take it back outside the orbit of Neptune, making it once again the farthest planet from the Sun.

The Planets

Planet	Diameter (in miles/ kilometers)	Distance from Sun (in miles/ kilometers)	Orbit Period (in Earth units)
Mercury	3,030/4,875	36,000,000/ 57,924,000	88 days
Venus	7,520/12,100	67,000,000/ 107,803,000	225 days
Earth	7,920/12,743	93,000,000/ 149,637,000	365 days
Mars	4,220/6,790	142,000,000/ 228,478,000	687 days
Jupiter	88,750/142,799	484,000,000/ 778,756,000	12 years
Saturn	74,560/119,967	890,000,000/ 1,432,010,000	29 years
Uranus	31,570/50,796	1,780,000,000/ 2,864,020,000	84 years
Neptune	30,200/48,592	2,790,000,000/ 4,489,110,000	165 years
Pluto	1,900/3,057	3,660,000,000/ 5,888,940,000	248 years

Pluto is still very much a mystery to astronomers. Because it is so far away, scientists have not been able to learn as much about it as they have about the other planets. Pluto is about two-thirds the size of Earth's moon, and is about 3,660 million miles (5,900 million kilometers) from the Sun. Because of its distance from the Sun, its year is equal to about 248 Earth years. Pluto's surface is covered with a layer of methane ice, but when its orbit brings it close to the Sun, some of this ice evaporates and a temporary atmosphere is produced.

Rotation Period (in Earth units)	Surface Temperature	Gravity (x Earth's)	Number of Moons	Composition	Atmosphere
59 days	-292 to 800°F (-180 to 427°C)	0.38	0	Iron and nickel core, rocky surface.	Very thin, mostly hydrogen and helium.
243 days	848 to 908°F (453 to 487°C)	0.91	0	Iron and nickel core, rocky surface.	Very dense, mostly carbon dioxide.
24 hours	-130 to 136°F (-90 to 58°C)	1	1	Iron and nickel core, water-covered surface.	Mostly nitrogen and oxygen.
24¼ hours	-190 to 80°F (-123 to 27°C)	0.38	2	Iron core, rocky surface.	Thin, mostly carbon dioxide.
10 hours	-238 to -148°F (-150 to -94°C)	2.5	16	Small, rocky core.	Layered, mostly hydrogen.
10 hours	-292 to -249°F (-180 to -156°C)	1.07	18	Small, rocky core.	Extensive, mostly hydrogen and helium.
13 to 24 hours	-330°F (-201°C)	0.93	15	Rock and ice core.	Hydrogen, helium, and methane.
18 hours	-306°F (-188°C)	1.2	8	Rock and ice core.	Hydrogen, helium, and methane.
6 days	-351°F (-213°C)	0.03	1	Unknown core.	Very thin, methane.

OPPOSITE, TOP: NEPTUNE WAS NAMED AFTER THE ROMAN GOD OF THE SEA, PROBABLY BECAUSE OF ITS PALE-BLUE COLOR. LEFT: A COMPUTER-GENERATED ILLUSTRATION OF PLUTO (LEFT) AND ITS MOON, CHARON (RIGHT).

A VIEW FROM APOLLO 11, THE SPACESHIP THAT FIRST CARRIED HUMANS TO THE MOON, AS IT FLIES OVER THE FAR SIDE OF THE MOON. EARTH IS VISIBLE IN THE BACKGROUND, ABOVE SOME OF THE MOON'S MANY CRATERS.

The Moon's Image

The Moon has fascinated human beings from the beginning of time. The world's different cultures have seen many different images in the Moon's bright face. The Yakuts of Siberia saw an image of a girl carrying two buckets on a pole across her shoulders; the Shan people of Burma perceived a silver hare; and the Inuits of the Arctic imagined a Man in the Moon who had a number of different masks that he changed often. What image do you see?

Moonless Nights

Only two planets in our solar system do not seem to have moons: Mercury and Venus. The Earth has one moon, which we call simply the Moon. Mars has two small moons, Deimos and Phobos, which at one time were probably asteroids. These asteroids may have traveled too close to Mars and been trapped in its gravitational pull. Jupiter has sixteen moons, five of which are named and eleven of which are known only by a number, and Saturn has at least eighteen.

MOONS

Moons, which are also referred to as **natural satellites,** are celestial bodies that orbit planets. Many of the solar system's planets have satellites. Earth has only one of these satellites, called the Moon, but some of the other planets have many. Saturn, for instance, has at least eighteen moons traveling in orbit around it.

Like the Earth's moon, many of the moons in the solar system are cold rocks that have no atmosphere, no water, and low gravity. With little or no atmosphere to trap and spread the heat from the Sun, the surface temperatures on some moons can change dramatically from day to night. For example, there can be a 500°F (about 260°C) difference between the day and night temperatures on Earth's moon.

Astronomers believe that at least some of the moons may have originally come from the planets they now orbit: a large object may have collided with the planet hard enough to break off a piece of the planet; this chunk of planet may then have become trapped by the planet's gravity and pulled into orbit around the planet. Another theory is that many of the moons may once have been large asteroids that passed close enough to a planet to be trapped in orbit by its gravity. It has not yet been determined whether either of these theories applies to Earth's moon.

The surfaces of many moons have large and small **craters**, which were created when objects from space crashed onto the moons' surfaces. On the Earth's moon, there are craters of many different sizes—one crater, for instance, is as large as the state of Texas. On some moons in our solar system, such as Io, one of Jupiter's moons, and Titan, a satellite of Neptune, craters disappear soon after they are created. This is because these moons have active volcanoes, and the lava that flows out of these volcanoes fills in the craters and smooths out the surfaces of the moons.

Some moons are covered with ice. Europa, another of Jupiter's moons, has a layer of ice covering its surface that is about 60 miles (96 kilometers) thick. In the pictures we have of this moon, it looks like a giant billiard ball with long lines crisscrossing its surface. The icy surface of Callisto, also a satellite of Jupiter, bears the mark of a giant meteorite. When this

Circular Craters

To find out how craters form and why they are always round, try creating your own craters on a make-believe planet surface. Ask an adult to help you with this experiment. You will need a newspaper, a large bowl or deep baking pan, all-purpose baking flour, cinnamon, small round objects (such as BBs, frozen peas, ball bearings, marbles, or small rubber balls), and tweezers.

1. Unfold the newspaper and place it on the floor or a table, then set the bowl or pan on top of the newspaper. Pour the flour into the bowl until you have a layer that is at least three or four inches thick (about 8 or 10 centimeters), then smooth out the flour until it is flat and even. Next, dust the top of the flour with cinnamon. The flour represents the Earth's interior; the cinnamon represents its crust.

2. Holding one of the small, round objects a few inches above the planet's surface, drop it. (The small round object acts like a meteorite crashing into the planet.)

3. Using tweezers, gently pull the "meteorite" out of the cinnamon and flour and look at the shape of the crater caused by its impact. How were the cinnamon and flour affected?

4. Smooth out the surface and try again, using different speeds and different angles.

5. When you are done experimenting with the meteorites, help clean up the mess you made.

DURING A LUNAR ECLIPSE, EARTH'S SHADOW SEEMS TO SWALLOW UP THE MOON.

DURING A SOLAR ECLIPSE, THE MOON MAY COMPLETELY BLOCK THE SUN—ALL THAT REMAINS VISIBLE IS THE SUN'S CORONA.

space rock crashed into Callisto, the icy surface probably melted, churned into waves, and then re-froze. The frozen waves now surround the mete-orite's point of impact.

Astronomers still have a great deal to learn about the moons in our solar sys-tem; as they continue their research, they may even dis-cover that the solar system has more moons than we currently know about. Earth's moon has always fascinated people. Because

of its motion through the sky, the changes in its appearance during each month, and the extraordi-nary events that it causes (such as **eclipses**), the Moon has been an important part of many cultures' religions and folklore.

There are many myths and legends about the Moon's effects on people and on the planet. And there have been just as many ideas about what the Moon looks like—to some people, it is an old man; to others, a long-eared rabbit.

The appearance of the Moon changes, though, from night to night. This is because our view of the "bright side" of the Moon changes as this satellite orbits Earth. The bright side of the Moon (which, con-trary to what many people believe, is not always the same side) is the part of the Moon that faces the Sun. When the entirety of the

bright side is facing Earth, we see a **full moon**, and when the entirety of the bright side is facing away from Earth, we see (or do not see) a dark moon, called the **new moon**. In between the full and the new moon are an almost full moon, called the **gib-bous moon**; a half moon, called the **quarter moon** (because we are seeing one-half of the bright side, which is actually only one-quarter of the Moon); and

IF YOU WATCH THE MOON OVER A PERIOD OF MANY NIGHTS, YOU WILL SEE IT CHANGE SHAPE. THESE CHANGING SHAPES ARE CALLED PHASES. ABOVE ARE SOME OF THESE PHASES (FROM LEFT TO RIGHT): CRESCENT, QUARTER, GIBBOUS, FULL.

Moon Shapes

The Moon makes one complete orbit of the Earth every 29½ days. As it travels, it seems to change shape. To learn why this happens, pretend that you are the Earth and that a ball, orange, or grapefruit is the Moon making its orbit around you. For this experiment, you need to be in a room that is dark except for one bright, uncovered light that you will use as the Sun.

1. Place yourself about five feet (1.5 meters) from the light; turn to one side, pointing one shoulder to the light; and hold your "moon" out in front of you. The side of the "moon" that is facing the light should be lit up and the side facing away should be in shadow. What shape do you see? Do you see what looks like a full moon? a half moon? a quarter moon?

2. To re-create the movements of the Moon around the Earth, move your "moon" around you while keeping your eye on it. (Keep your body still and your arm at the same level.) You should see the lit-up area of your "moon" change shape. In what position do you see the full moon (when the Moon appears as a full circle)? the dark new moon (when you can't see the Moon at all)?

3. After you have let your "moon" orbit you a few times, try making a solar eclipse. Place the "moon" between you and the bright light. A solar eclipse occurs when the Moon comes between the Earth and the Sun, briefly blocking the Sun's light and creating a shadow on part of the Earth.

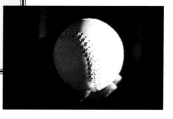

a sliver of the Moon, called the **crescent moon**. These different shapes are called the Moon's **phases**. When the Moon is approaching full (getting larger) it is said to be **waxing**, and when it is approaching new (getting smaller) it is said to be **waning**.

Occasionally, when the Moon comes between the Earth and the Sun, the Moon casts a shadow on Earth. (In the same way that you cast a shadow on the sidewalk or the ground when you are outside, Earth and the Moon cast shadows into space.) This event is called a **solar eclipse**, and for a small part of Earth it can make the middle of the day seem like early evening as the light from the Sun is blocked by the Moon. An eclipse of this kind lasts for only a few minutes, but it is quite spectacular. Remember, however, *never* to look directly at the Sun, because you can seriously damage your eyes. If you really want to view an eclipse, ask a

local astronomer about the safest way to do so.

Sometimes, Earth will cast its shadow over the Moon. This is called a **lunar eclipse**. The Native American Cherokee believed that when this happened, the Moon was being swallowed up by a giant frog. But do not worry—lunar eclipses are short-lived phenomena. From a few minutes to a little over an hour after the Moon is covered, it will reappear on the other side of Earth's shadow.

ASTEROIDS, METEORS, AND COMETS

Between Mars and Jupiter, there is a strip, or band, of thousands of small and large rocks in orbit around the Sun. These rocks are called asteroids (which means "starlike"), and this strip of asteroids is called the **asteroid belt**. Asteroids come in many different sizes and shapes. Some, such as Ceres, which is 600 miles (966 kilometers) across, are quite large; others are very small. Even though some are large, all the asteroids combined would still be smaller than Earth's moon.

Astronomers believe that asteroids are occasionally knocked out of their orbits and drift into space. Any

**ABOUT THE ONLY WAY THAT
SCIENTISTS CAN PHYSICALLY EXAM-
INE SPACE MATERIAL IS BY STUDY-
ING METEORITES LIKE THIS ONE.**

drifting chunks of rock are called **meteoroids**. When meteoroids drift toward Earth and fall into its atmosphere, they are called **meteors**. As meteors fall to Earth, they reach speeds of up to 25 miles (40 kilometers) per second; as a result, most of them burn up before they hit the ground. Those that do not burn up are called **meteorites**.

Throughout history, there have been many mete-orites, of varying size, that

have landed on the surface of the Earth. Scientists have found evidence that a particularly large meteorite crashed to Earth 65 million years ago, and some scientists believe that it was the impact of this meteorite that caused the extinction of the dinosaurs.

Asteroids and meteors, however, are not the only travelers in our solar system. **Comets** are frozen balls of ice and dust that are trapped in very large orbits around a star.

Scientists believe that comets were originally part of the donut-shaped cloud of material that surrounded the Sun billions of years ago, when it was young. Within this cloud there were many collisions, and some objects were probably knocked out of the cloud

Shooting Stars

The "shooting stars" that we are all familiar with are actually meteors. As they burn up in the atmosphere, they leave behind them a trail of light, which quickly disappears. Occasionally, the Earth travels through an area of space that has a lot of cosmic dust. (Almost a ton [0.9 metric tons] of cosmic dust falls to Earth every day.) This dust enters the Earth's atmosphere and burns up, giving us a **meteor shower**. During a meteor shower there may be more than fifty shooting stars each minute.

and into orbit around the Sun. These objects became comets.

Comets' orbits vary widely. For instance, Halley's Comet comes near the Earth about every seventy-six years, while some comets have orbits that are so large that it may take them thousands of years to orbit the Sun. When a comet's orbit brings it near Earth, the comet can be seen in the sky as a slow-moving star. (In fact, when early peoples saw comets in the sky, they often believed them to be omens of evil or ill fortune.) While comets seem to shine with a light of their own, they are in fact only reflecting the Sun's light. Comet "tails" are made up of gases and dust that are given off as the Sun warms the comets. The tails of some comets may reach millions of miles (kilometers) into space.

THE GASEOUS TAILS OF COMETS ARE OFTEN VERY BRIGHT. IF A LARGE COMET COMES CLOSE ENOUGH TO EARTH, IT MAY BE VISIBLE DURING THE DAY AS WELL AS AT NIGHT.

CHAPTER FOUR

EXPLORATION

AN ADVERTISEMENT FOR THE 1902 MOVIE *A TRIP TO THE MOON*, WHICH WAS BASED ON THE JULES VERNE NOVEL *FROM THE EARTH TO THE MOON*.

Is There Life out There?

Does the energy from the Sun support life on other planets? Astronomers and other scientists have been studying the other planets for centuries in an effort to answer this and other questions, but to date no evidence of life has been found.

Space travel is an age-old dream. It is exciting to imagine oneself flying from planet to planet and from star to star in search of answers to such age-old mysteries as "How large is the universe?" or "Is there intelligent life in outer space?" Science fiction literature and movies let our imaginations explore the universe while our bodies stay on Earth. While most people think of science fiction as a relatively new subject, people have in fact been making up science fiction stories for centuries. For example, the ancient Greek storyteller Lucian Samasata, who lived more than 1,500 years ago, created a story about a sailing ship that was caught in a whirlwind and flew to the Moon. There have been many inventive science fiction stories that seemed to predict the future. In 1865 the French novelist Jules Verne wrote a story about a trip to the Moon; only about one hundred years later, two U.S. astronauts took the first steps on the Moon. What was once science fiction has become science fact, and there are now a growing number of true stories about machines and people that have traveled beyond the confines of our planet.

TAKING A PEEK

Astronomers such as **Galileo Galilei** and **Isaac Newton**, both of whom lived hundreds of years ago, were among the first people to use **telescopes** to look more closely at the wonders of the sky. The first telescope was invented in 1608 by a Dutch optician named Hans Lippershey. Galileo found out about this device and in 1609 built one of his own, which he later improved upon. This instrument was a **refracting telescope**, which uses a series of glass lenses to magnify, or enlarge, the image of the object being observed. (This kind of telescope is still commonly used today.) Although Galileo's telescope had only about as much magnification power as a pair of modern binoculars, he was still able to make some wonderful discoveries. Later in the 1600s, Isaac Newton invented the **reflecting telescope**, which uses mirrors to magnify images.

BELOW: GALILEO GALILEI. BOTTOM: ISAAC NEWTON'S REFLECTING TELESCOPE. INSET: NEWTON WITH A PRISM.

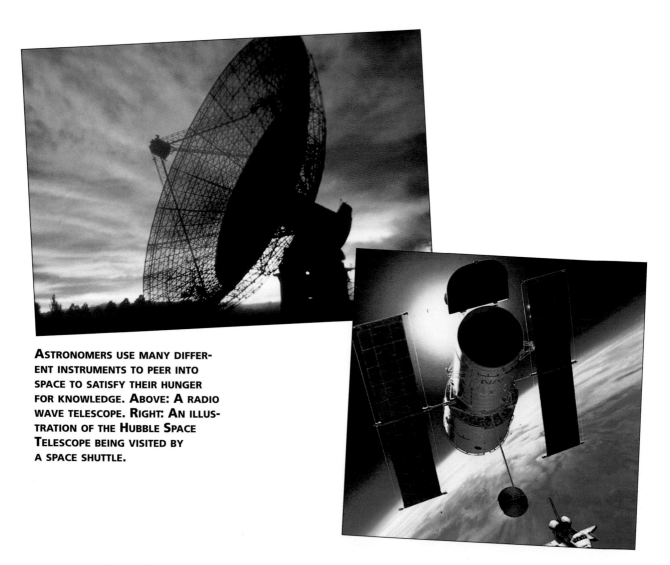

**ASTRONOMERS USE MANY DIFFER-
ENT INSTRUMENTS TO PEER INTO
SPACE TO SATISFY THEIR HUNGER
FOR KNOWLEDGE. ABOVE: A RADIO
WAVE TELESCOPE. RIGHT: AN ILLUS-
TRATION OF THE HUBBLE SPACE
TELESCOPE BEING VISITED BY
A SPACE SHUTTLE.**

Since Newton's time, scientists have made many improvements in telescope technology and invented a number of new instruments for observing faraway objects and collecting data about them. Today's astronomers have many different kinds of instruments for research. One of the most important of these new devices is the **radio wave telescope**, which collects radio waves instead of light waves (refracting and reflecting telescopes work by gathering light). Scientists believe that if there is intelligent life in other parts of our galaxy, we may one day be able to hear signs of their existence with our radio telescopes. So far, though, no one has heard any alien broadcasts.

Another important tool that has recently been developed is the **Hubble Space Telescope**, which was launched into orbit around Earth in 1990. Because this telescope is far above Earth's atmosphere (which tends to have a distorting effect on images of objects beyond it), scientists are now able to view distant objects much more clearly. The Hubble Space Telescope, which is scheduled to remain in orbit until around 2005, also carries instruments that allow it to measure the precise positions of stars, analyze the chemical make-up of stars and galaxies, and measure the brightness of faraway objects.

A MODEL OF THE SOVIET SATELLITE *SPUTNIK 1* ON DISPLAY AT THE NATIONAL AIR AND SPACE MUSEUM IN WASHINGTON, D.C.

A Full Sky

There are hundreds of satellites in orbit around Earth. Unfortunately, some of these satellites break apart in orbit and the small pieces of debris created by their breaking apart travel around Earth. There are now so many satellites and pieces of satellites in orbit that soon many will collide with each other. This could start a chain reaction of collisions that would destroy many satellites and make it very dangerous for astronauts to be in orbit around Earth.

REACHING OUT

In 1957 the former Soviet Union launched the first artificial satellite, called *Sputnik 1*. This small machine weighed 184 pounds (83.5 kilograms) and was only 2 feet (0.6 meters) wide, but it stirred a lot of interest and sparked a race in the exploration of outer space. The United States and the Soviet Union began launching satellite after satellite into orbit around the Earth. Many of these satellites were designed for investigating the atmosphere and weather, while others were designed for military purposes.

In 1961 the Soviet Union launched the first planetary probe, called *Venera 1*. It was aimed toward Venus, but missed that planet by 60,000 miles (96,500 kilometers). A year later, the United States launched the first successful planetary probe, *Mariner 2*, which was able to fly much closer to Venus (it came within 21,594 miles [about 34,745 kilometers] of the planet) and send back information about its hot atmosphere. Since then, numerous planetary probes have flown to other planets and sent back information about their atmospheres and surfaces.

STEPPING OUT

The ultimate goal of the space programs was to launch human beings into space. On April 12, 1961, **Yuri Gagarin**, a Soviet **astronaut,** became the first person to reach orbit around Earth. In a space-craft known as *Vostok 1* he made one orbit around our planet and saw two sunrises. From this time on, U.S. and Soviet space flights grew longer and longer.

Small Heroes

The first successful space-flight for live creatures was achieved by the United States in 1951, when it launched a rocket carrying a monkey and eleven mice. After a short flight and a safe landing, the animals were recovered alive and well.

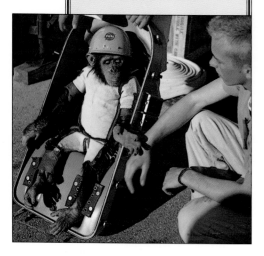

Escaping the Force

To escape the Earth's gravitational pull, vehicles must be moving at a speed of at least 7 miles (11.2 kilometers) per second, which is equal to 25,000 miles (40,000 kilometers) per hour. These machines are pushed into space by rockets, which use lots of fuel. Because of this, ships sent into space are designed as large fuel tanks with big engines and only a small compartment for the cargo and passengers.

Walking in Space

In 1965 Ed White became the first U.S. citizen to "walk" in space. During the *Gemini 4* mission, he stepped out of his space capsule (he was attached to the capsule by a long strap that was very strong). Using a handheld power pack nicknamed a Zot Gun, White was able to move around outside the ship.

The next step was to send a person to the Moon. On July 20, 1969, American astronauts **Neil Armstrong** and **Edwin "Buzz" Aldrin** took the first walk on the Moon. This was a milestone in the history of the space program—a dream come true—and millions of people watched the historic event on their television sets. The astronauts collected data about the Moon's rocks, craters, and other features. When the astronauts returned to Earth, they were treated as heroes.

U.S. ASTRONAUT BUZZ ALDRIN WITH THE METAL U.S. FLAG EMBEDDED IN THE SURFACE OF THE MOON. THE FOOTPRINTS THAT ALDRIN AND HIS PARTNER, NEIL ARMSTRONG, LEFT ON THE MOON WILL PROBABLY BE THERE FOREVER.

How Does a Spaceship Fly?

When rocket fuel burns, it pushes down and out of the rocket. The rocket is then pushed up and away from the launch pad. This reaction is explained by **Newton's Third Law of Motion**, which states that for every action there is an equal and opposite reaction. You can use a balloon to test this principle. If you blow up a balloon, leaving the end untied, then let go of it, the balloon will fly through the air away from you. This is because the air inside the balloon is under pressure. When you let go of the mouth of the balloon, the pressure forces air out of the balloon, and the balloon is pushed in the opposite direction from the opening.

After the success of the efforts to send people to the Moon, the space agencies of the world set their sights even higher. One of of the new goals was to build **space stations**, large residential and research centers that would be built in orbit around Earth, the Moon, or some other celestial body.

In 1971 the Soviet Union launched *Salyut 1*, the first space station. Soon after, in 1973, the National Aeronautics and Space Administration (NASA), the agency that heads the U.S. space program, launched its first space station, *Skylab 1*. These and other space stations helped better our understanding of what it might mean to live and work in space.

NASA's **space shuttle** program was another important component of the exploration of space. The shuttles are vehicles that are designed to be launched into space many times, carrying cargo into orbit and sometimes returning with new cargo, such as damaged satellites. In combination with the space stations, the shuttles are intended to allow

SKYLAB 1 (BELOW) AND THE SPACE SHUTTLE *DISCOVERY* (RIGHT) ON THE LAUNCH PAD.

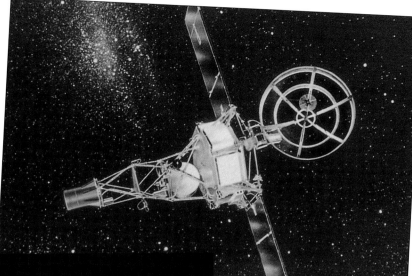

ILLUSTRATIONS OF TWO PLANETARY PROBES: *MARINER 2* (RIGHT) AND *VOYAGER 2* (BELOW). IT TOOK *VOYAGER 2* TWELVE YEARS TO REACH ITS DESTINATION: THE PLANET NEPTUNE.

Remote Eyes

The machines we launch into space often send back surprising information. A probe named *Voyager 2* visited Neptune in 1989. The instruments on this probe revealed to astronomers that Neptune had more than the two moons that we could see with our telescopes—it actually has eight moons.

scientists to explore the solar system in many new ways. (For instance, the Hubble Space Telescope was launched from a space shuttle).

NASA's first successful space shuttle, *Columbia,* left the launch pad on April 12, 1981, with an empty cargo bay and made thirty-six orbits around Earth before landing safely in California fifty-four hours later. Since then, the space agencies of the Soviet Union, the United States, and other countries have all contributed greatly to our understanding of the solar system and the regions beyond.

THE FUTURE

There are many ways in which we can continue to explore our solar system. As our technology improves, so will our ability to send both machine and human farther into space. The continuing development of space stations may be just the first step to having people live permanently outside of Earth's atmosphere.

To date, the farthest humans have traveled has been to the Moon. Half a century ago this was only a dream—science fiction—but in time this dream came true. How many of today's dreams will come true? It seems likely that people may one day live in space

Living in Space

Because there is no gravity in space, astronauts who remain away from Earth for prolonged periods must change many of their habits. They must exercise regularly in order to keep strong; otherwise, their muscles and bones will weaken because of the lack of gravity. Eating is a challenge—food just floats away if the astronauts are not careful. And sleeping is not easy either; astronauts must strap themselves to a wall in order to prevent themselves from floating around in the cabin.

SPACE STATIONS ARE DESIGNED IN ALL KINDS OF SHAPES AND SIZES. IN THIS CONCEPTUAL DRAWING, SOLAR COLLECTORS STRETCH OUT TO GATHER THE SUN'S ENERGY.

stations around other planets, and perhaps even in colonies on the surfaces of other planets. They might mine for minerals, trade with Earth, and conduct research to help further our understanding of the solar system and of outer space in general.

A **space colony** would most likely be run in much the same way that towns and cities are run. There would of course be scientists, but there would also be tradespeople, shopkeepers, businesspeople, and even politicians. The colony would need a constant supply of fresh food, so there would need to be one or more large gardens. The people would probably not have to wear spacesuits, as the colony would have a dome or other structure specially designed to keep out harmful radiation and keep in an artificial atmosphere. All in all, except for the view out the window, life in a space colony would probably be very much like life here on Earth.

It is uncertain how quickly we will learn about all that is to be found in outer space, but it is certain that there are still many wonderful things to discover about this small part of the universe called the solar system.

Plan a Space Colony

It is now time to use your newfound knowledge about the solar system and our exploration of it in a fun and creative way. Pretend you have been given the responsibility of designing a space colony on one of the other eight planets. You must decide who will live in this colony, what the buildings and vehicles will look like, and how everybody and everything will get there.

1. First, decide on a planet. Mars or Venus would probably be best, as they have firm, rocky surfaces on which buildings and roads can be built. Jupiter or Saturn, however, would be hard to colonize, as they have no solid surfaces, and colonies would therefore have to float.

2. Decide whether you are going to draw the colony or make models of it with building blocks, clay, or paper cutouts.

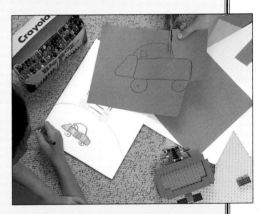

3. Design the spaceship that will take everything to the colony, then design the buildings and vehicles that will be built. What will it all look like? Will the buildings and cars look like buildings and cars we have on Earth? Why, or why not? Does the planet you chose have the same gravity as Earth, and does it matter? What about the surface temperature? Does it need to be hotter or cooler? Ask an adult to help you if you like. Good luck. The colonists are counting on you.

BIBLIOGRAPHY

Children's Books

Braus, Judy, ed. *Nature Scope: Astronomy Adventures*. Washington, D.C.: National Wildlife Federation, 1992.

Docekal, Eileen M. *Sky Detective*. New York: Sterling Publishing Co., 1992.

Estalella, Robert. *The Stars*. Hauppauge, N.Y.: Barron's, 1993.

Maynard, Christopher. *The Usborne Young Scientist: Stars and Planets*. London: Usborne Publishing Ltd., 1991.

Rey, H.A. *The Stars*. Boston: Houghton Mifflin Co., 1967.

Stott, Carole. *I Wonder Why Stars Twinkle*. New York: Kingfisher Books, 1993.

VanCleaves, Janice. *Astronomy for Every Kid*. New York: John Wiley and Sons, 1991.

Young Adult Books

Chartrand, Mark R. *A Golden Guide: Exploring Space*. Racine, Wis.: Golden Press, 1991.

_____. *Sky Guide: A Field Guide to the Heavens*. Racine, Wis.: Golden Press, 1990.

Engelbrekston, Sune. *Stars, Planets, and Galaxies*. New York: Grosset & Dunlap, 1975.

Gallant, Roy A. *The Planets: Exploring Our Solar System*. New York: Four Winds Press, 1989.

Lauber, Patricia. *Journey to the Planets*. New York: Crown Publishers, 1993.

Moore, Patrick. *The Universe for the Beginner*. New York: Press Syndicate of the University of Cambridge, 1990.

Muirden, James. *The Universe*. New York: Little Simon, 1987.

Ordway, Frederick I. III, and Randy Liebermann, eds. *Blueprint for Space*. Washington, D.C.: Smithsonian Institution Press, 1991.

Walter, William. *Space Age*. New York: Random House, 1992.

Magazines

Ad Astra
National Space Society
922 Pennsylvania Ave. SE
Washington, DC 20003

Astronomy
AstroMedia Corp.
P.O. Box 92788
Milwaukee, WI 53202

Aviation Week & Space Technology
P.O. Box 1505
Neptune, NJ 07753

Sky and Telescope
Sky Publishing Corp.
49 Bay State Rd.
Cambridge, MA 02138

Museums and Planetariums

American Museum—Hayden Planetarium
81st Street @ Central Park West
New York, NY 10024

Griffith Observatory and Planetarium
2800 East Observatory Rd.
Los Angeles, CA 90027

National Air and Space Museum
6th and Independence Ave. SW
Washington, DC 20560

Spaceport USA
Kennedy Space Center, FL 32899

INDEX

PHOTO CREDITS